Cryptic Canada

Unsolved Mysteries
from Coast to Coast

Written by **Natalie Hyde**

Illustrated by **Matt Hammill**

Owlkids Books Inc.
10 Lower Spadina Avenue, Suite 400, Toronto, Ontario M5V 2Z2
www.owlkidsbooks.com

Distributed in Canada by University of Toronto Press
5201 Dufferin Street, Toronto, Ontario M3H 5T8

Distributed in the United States by Publishers Group West
1700 Fourth Street, Berkeley, California 94710

Library and Archives Canada Cataloguing in Publication

Hyde, Natalie, 1963-
    Cryptic Canada : unsolved mysteries from coast to coast / written
by Natalie Hyde ; illustrated by Matt Hammill.

Includes index.
Issued also in an electronic format.
ISBN 978-1-926973-38-8 (bound).--ISBN 978-1-926973-43-2 (pbk.)

    1. Canada--Miscellanea--Juvenile literature. I. Hammill, Matt
II. Title.

FC58.H94 2012   j971   C2011-908321-3

Library of Congress Control Number: 2011944600

Design: Samantha Edwards and Barb Kelly

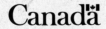

We acknowledge the financial support of the Canada Council for the Arts, the Ontario
Arts Council, the Government of Canada through the Canada Book Fund (CBF) and the
Government of Ontario through the Ontario Media Development Corporation's Book
Initiative for our publishing activities.

Printed in Shah Alam, Selangor Darul Ehsan, Malaysia, in May 2012
Job #227587

A   B   C   D   E   F

Publisher of Chirp, chickaDEE and OWL
www.owlkids.com

CONTENTS

Cryptic Canada

Unsolved Mysteries
from Coast to Coast

Written by **Natalie Hyde**

Illustrated by **Matt Hammill**

People travel to Egypt to marvel at mummies and pyramids, to Easter Island to see hundreds of monolithic figures, and to England to stand before the massive pillars of Stonehenge.

You might think you have to be a world traveller to see mystifying and wondrous creations of ancient peoples. But wait! Before you update your passport, you should know that some of the most mysterious and exciting sites exist someplace much closer to home—right here in Canada.

Mummies, pirates, and bootleggers? We've got 'em. Underground cities? You bet. Unexplained artifacts, astounding symbols, buried treasure? They're all right here.

We are about to go on a cross-country tour of our most enigmatic sites. We might even discover some things that will make it necessary to rewrite the history books by the time we're done. So leave your passport and suitcase at home and come discover *Cryptic Canada*.

CHAPTER ONE

Oak Island
Buried Treasure

History Mystery

Oak Island (bottom), off the south coast of Nova Scotia, is the site of the longest-running treasure hunt in history.

The sounds of huge drills and excavation machines fill the air. Another shaft is being dug on Oak Island, Nova Scotia. There are so many of these shafts on the east corner of the island that the earth here is a honeycomb of pits and holes.

What are people looking for? Buried treasure.

More than two hundred years ago, in 1795, a young man named Daniel McGinnis explored Oak Island and noticed a large section of sunken earth. The branch of a nearby oak tree hung over this site, and Daniel was sure he could see scuff marks on a branch. He thought the marks looked like those left behind by a block and tackle. A block and tackle is a simple machine that

Pirate-ship carpenters made emergency repairs in deserted coves using materials scavenged on shore.

uses ropes and pulleys to help people raise heavy items. This system is often used on sailing ships to help load and unload cargo.

Daniel wondered whether something heavy had been lowered into a pit in the ground and covered up. Maybe over time, the dirt used to fill in the hole had settled, causing the area to appear sunken compared to the land around it.

It was still big news in Nova Scotia that some of Captain Kidd's treasure, which included gold dust, bars of silver, Spanish dollars, rubies, and diamonds, had been found buried on New York's Gardiners Island in the 1690s. The rest of the treasure had never been found. Daniel had likely heard the rumours that Captain Kidd had buried more of his treasure along the east coast of North America. Could the treasure have been lowered into a pit on Oak Island?

Daniel grabbed two friends, John Smith and Anthony Vaughn, and some shovels, and they started digging. The dirt came out easily, and they could see pick marks all along the hardpacked walls of the shaft. This site had clearly been dug out and refilled before. The three men could barely contain their excitement. This was it! They were sure the treasure was within reach.

Every 3 m (10 ft.) or so, they hit a layer of oak timber, but they continued digging through these layers for just over 9 m (30 ft.), excited that they were soon to be rich. At this point the shaft became too deep to dig by hand and to continue would have required more than just shovels. They needed help. They had to put their treasure hunt on hold.

It took the three men several years, but eventually they found someone to invest money so they could hire more people to continue digging with steam-powered drills. Now they were making real progress. But one day, as it was getting dark, after they had reached down just over 30 m (100 ft.), the crew decided to quit for the day. The next morning, they discovered the pit was filled with water! They tried bailing it out, but they weren't able to empty the pit. They used a pump, but as quickly as they pumped the water out, it rushed in again. If the crew had hit a spring, the water would have seeped in slowly. This water filled the shaft so quickly they realized that deep below the ground, flood tunnels must be funnelling water into the shaft. This could only mean one thing...the pit was booby-trapped! They were not going to give up, though—one of the world's longest-running treasure hunts had begun.

Captain Kidd

The notorious Captain William Kidd was originally hired by the British to capture French ships and also to rid the sea of pirates. While on that job, he developed a taste for plundering ships, looting treasure, and even committing murder. When he sailed to New York with a captured ship full of treasure, he thought he would be hailed as a hero. But in the eyes of the British government, he had become the worst kind of pirate. In 1701, he was tried and hanged for his crimes.

The Money Pit

0.7 m (2 ft.) A layer of flat stones not usually found on Oak Island. This type of stone is typically found near Gold River, about 3 km (2 mi.) away.

3 m (10 ft.) Oak platforms every 3 m (10 ft.). The soil underneath each layer of wood had settled, making an empty space about 30 to 60 cm (1 to 2 ft.) deep.

11 m (36 ft.) Sea level. Water rose to this level when the pit flooded.

33 m (108 ft.) The flood tunnel. As soon as excavators reached this level, water rushed in, filling the hole.

46.6 m (153 ft.) Drill struck an iron plate.

52.1 m (171 ft.) Drill struck a layer of soft stone, a layer of oak, then loose metal and parchment. The drill brought up a small piece of parchment with a handwritten letter V or R on it.

The original shaft is difficult to recognize now due to numerous excavations, including attempts to destroy the flood tunnel with dynamite.

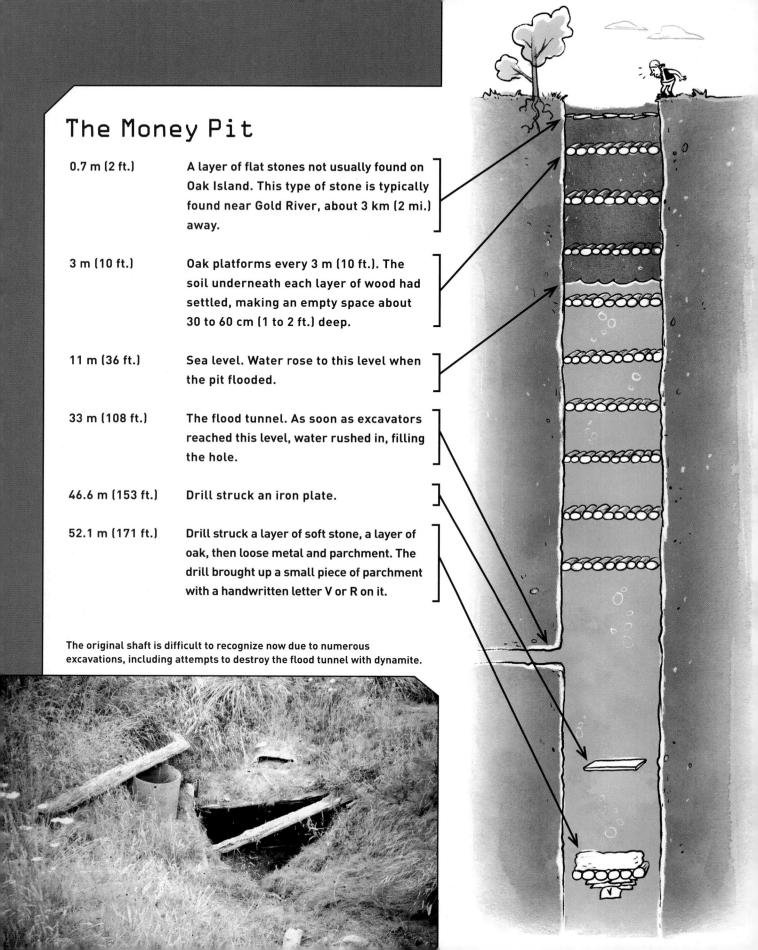

Treasure hunters tried to build temporary dams (below) to hold back the water from the flood tunnel but were unsuccessful.

Puzzle Pieces

By watching the water rise and fall with the tides, the searchers determined that the flood tunnel brought water in from nearby Smith's Cove. When the treasure hunters investigated the cove, they discovered something amazing. Mysterious engineers had not only rigged a booby-trapped pit but had also built an entire false beach!

Searchers dug down to try to block the flood tunnel. When they dug through the sand and gravel beach, they found a thick layer of coconut fibre. But the nearest coconut tree is about 2,500 km (1,500 mi.) south of Oak Island! How did fibre end up at Smith's Cove?

Under the coconut fibre is a layer of eelgrass, then a layer of stones. These layers act like a strainer that keeps out sand, clay, and leaves so that the drains and flood tunnel underneath don't clog. The fact that each material is in a separate layer leads researchers to believe they were placed there on purpose. If this were a natural structure, these materials would be mixed together, with no clear separation, as the tides wash in and out.

The false beach funnels water into five finger-like drains. These drains connect to each other somewhere deep underground to form the flood tunnel that keeps the shaft full of water no matter how hard treasure hunters dig. It is a masterful design. If one or more of the beach drains were to get clogged or destroyed, water from the others would still flood the shaft.

Clearly, someone has gone to a lot of trouble to make sure that the treasure cannot be easily found.

Pirate Proof?

An iron ruler was found at Smith's Cove. It was forged and engraved by hand. Researchers studying the metal say it was made before 1783. Was it lost by someone building the false beach?

A diver attempting to retrieve items from the pit barely escaped when the lower walls of the shaft collapsed.

What Now?

In 1971, a company called Triton Alliance sunk a new shaft, northeast of the original pit that Daniel McGinnis discovered, called Borehole 10X. Between 40 and 50 m (140 and 160 ft.) down, they found bits of brass, china, and wood.

At 72 m (235 ft.) down, the shaft widened, and the crew lowered a camera into the water-filled cavern. Newspapers reported that in the murky water, researchers saw what looked like a human hand cut off at the wrist and three wooden chests. Divers were lowered into the cavern, but it was too dangerous to explore.

Excavations on Oak Island continue today. Oak Island Tours is the company that manages the digs, and the company's team is working hard to find ways around the flood tunnel so they can solve the mystery of what is buried on the island.

Oak Island Tours has hired a marine technology firm that uses sidescan sonar to map objects on the ocean floor. Several of these images show unusual formations around Oak Island. Nature does not usually produce right angles, especially with rocks where sharp edges are eroded by wind, ice, or water. When researchers see sharp or right angles, they take a closer look to see if the object was made by humans. Several of the sonar images show a rectangular object on the ocean floor. So far, the searchers haven't determined what it is, but many of them believe it could be a treasure chest. Oak Island Tours is also doing an electrical resistivity study. In the same way that sonar uses sound waves to see under water, this method uses the flow of electricity to map features under the ground.

Ask an Expert

NAME: Charles Barkhouse
TITLE: Historian
FROM: Friends of Oak Island

Can anyone dig for the treasure?

Most of Oak Island is private property, so visitors to the island cannot dig for treasure. Also, anyone excavating must have a valid Treasure Trove licence from the government. Getting this licence can take a long time because the person applying has to pay for studies of the site and soil when they apply. The licence is only good for one year and then the whole process has to be repeated.

Is the false beach at Smith's Cove still being investigated?

Not at this time, but you would need special permits to excavate Smith's Cove now.

Do the treasure hunters believe there is pirate treasure buried there?

When Daniel McGinnis first started digging, it was thought to be pirate treasure because in those days, pirates were known to have used rivers and coves in Nova Scotia to repair their ships. It was also easier to get people to invest their money with such a story because it seemed very possible. Now there are many theories about what could be buried there. One thing is certain: someone or some group went through a great deal of trouble to bury something of great value.

What will happen to the treasure if it is found?

It depends on what is found there. If it is something like gold bars, coins, gems, or jewellery, the finder or finders would be able to keep most of it after giving a percentage to the government. If it is artwork or religious artifacts or documents, the government might keep it because it has historical or cultural significance.

CHAPTER TWO

Ice Mummies
of the Arctic

History Mystery

The man with the red cloth wrapped around his head needs a shave. His scraggly beard can't hide how thin his face is, though, and his smile reveals a mouth full of decayed teeth. Clearly he isn't in the best shape. But he doesn't look bad for someone who has been dead for 140 years.

This man is William Braine, one of three ice mummies found on Beechey Island in the Northwest Territories. Braine, John Torrington, and John Hartnell were sailing with Sir John Franklin as he tried to find the Northwest Passage in 1845. The three men died early in the voyage and were buried on the rocky beach.

Water seeped into their coffins and never thawed. The ice that formed preserved the men so perfectly that when scientists found them, Hartnell's dark hair was still tucked up under his cap and Torrington's blue eyes stared back at them. After the deaths of these three men, the rest of the crew voyaged on. But in 1846, Franklin's two ships, the *Terror* and the *Erebus*, and both their crews simply vanished.

The navy wool cloth that covered John Torrington's face in his coffin dyed his forehead and nose blue.

The three graves, each with an inscribed wooden marker, were found on Beechey Island in 1850 by Elisha Kane, during his search for Franklin's ships.

In 1850, four years after the crews went missing, the site of their winter camp was discovered on Beechey Island, along with the three icy graves. But there were no signs of the ships, the captain, or the crew members. Five years later, a search party found a clue: in a cairn (a mound of stones) on nearby King William Island in Nunavut, there were messages from some of the last survivors. There, the search party found not only more graves, but also skeletons, scattered all over the ground and under an overturned boat. These people had not even been buried.

Altogether, Sir John Franklin made four trips into the Canadian Arctic, mapping more than 4,800 km (3,000 mi.) of coastline.

Scientists examined the mummies on Beechey Island for clues explaining what happened to the expedition. Forensic tests gave some surprising answers about the doomed voyage, but Sir John Franklin's body and the two ships have not been found to this day.

An Ongoing Investigation

After defrosting John Hartnell's mummy, forensic anthropologist Dr. Owen Beattie was shocked to discover that the body had already been autopsied...150 years earlier. It seems that the doctor on Franklin's expedition had opened up John Hartnell for the same reason Dr. Beattie had—to learn why these sailors died so early in the expedition.

Teeth marks on William Braine's shoulders tell a gruesome tale. He wasn't buried immediately after his death, and rats began to gnaw at his body.

Puzzle Pieces

The ice mummies allow researchers to study something that skeletons do not: tissue. Scientists have tested the men's tissues for clues as to what killed them so early in their voyage. Finding out what happened to these three men could help the scientists answer questions about what happened to the rest of the crew members and to Franklin himself.

All three men were very thin when they died. But wouldn't it have been too early in the trip for them to be starving? The Franklin Expedition was one of the first to use the newly invented tin can to store its food supply, and the crew had packed enough canned food to last several years.

Searching for an explanation, scientists took samples of the mummies' hairs, fingernails, and bones. They made a shocking discovery: the men had been poisoned! The level of lead in their bodies was over a hundred times higher than that normally recorded in a healthy human.

The researchers suspected the tin cans were the source of the poisoning. Lead had been used to solder the cans shut, and maybe it had leeched into the food inside. If so, then every meal on the ship would have been potentially fatal. Each spoonful would have contributed to more and more brain and nerve damage so that the explorers wouldn't be able to think clearly.

Many crew members left the ships in April 1848 and tried to walk south to find shelter and a way home, but they used very poor judgment. The only official record found on King William Island was a form stuffed inside the rocks of a cairn. The document was mainly a progress report from 28 May 1847, and ended with "All's well." Another entry, though, had been scribbled in the margins. It was dated one year later and stated that Sir John Franklin had died only two weeks after the first entry. The two ships had been trapped in ice for a year and a half, and the remaining crew of 105 men was abandoning the ships.

Franklin ordered 8,000 tins of soups, meats, and vegetables for the journey. The supplier, rushing because he was behind schedule, let the lead solder leak through the seams that sealed the cans, contaminating the food inside.

The crew planned to walk to Back River, the last entry noted. But the mental confusion from the lead poisoning may have been the cause of their ultimate demise. As well as trying to drag a twelve thousand–pound boat with them, they had filled it with a bizarre collection of items, including silk handkerchiefs, hair combs, books, perfumed soap, and slippers—none of the things they would need to make a safe trip in the wintry landscape.

While the men who were mummified had been buried in graves with marked headstones, at camp, some skeletons were found in tents, while others were scattered on the ground, left to decompose where they dropped. On top of that, there was evidence that some members of the crew had turned to cannibalism.

Dr. John Rae, who worked for the Hudson's Bay Company, was one of the first rescuers to go looking for Franklin's crew. He met some Inuit hunters who told him of a group of men they had seen eating human flesh. When Rae reported this news to the British government, they were outraged. They couldn't believe that British officers would engage in this kind of behaviour.

It wasn't until 1992 that evidence of cannibalism was found. Archaeologist Margaret Bertulli and anthropologist Anne Keenleyside studied more than four hundred human bones found on the island using a scanning electron microscope and they discovered many cuts on the bones that had been made by the crew's blades, not animal teeth.

Lead Poisoning

Lead is a soft metal that has been mined and used for thousands of years. It has often been used in water pipes, bullets, and beads. But lead is poisonous to animals, including humans. Since the 1970s, governments have banned the use of lead in paint and gasoline to reduce the risk of health problems in humans. People suffering from severe lead poisoning have difficulty with their memory and concentration. They may experience headaches, trouble sleeping, depression, and even hallucinations. Lead also interferes with the immune system, making it easier for other diseases to take hold. If the level of lead continues to increase in a person's body, the victim can slip into a coma. Those who survive lead poisoning often have permanent brain damage.

What Now?

In 1992, researchers looked for the two shipwrecks south of King William Island using a magnetometer. This device measures magnetic fields under water. They found several spots that looked a little like the shape of a ship, but when researchers dropped sonar equipment through holes in the ice, they didn't discover anything there. So far the ships are nowhere to be found.

In July 2010, researchers found a ship they hadn't been looking for: the *Investigator*, which had been sent to look for the Franklin Expedition in 1850 and had also become icebound. The crew of the *Investigator* was lucky enough to have been rescued in 1853 after spending four terrible and fruitless winters in the Arctic.

Even though the two ships from the Franklin Expedition have not yet been found, both the *Terror* and the *Erebus* have been named National Historic Sites of Canada.

A team of researchers studies the ruins of Northumberland House on King William Island. This house was a wooden supply depot set up by one of the last teams to search for the members of the lost Franklin Expedition.

Ask an Expert

NAME: Dr. Owen Beattie
TITLE: Professor Emeritus
FROM: University of Alberta
Author of *Frozen in Time: The Fate of the Franklin Expedition*

What was the hardest part about examining the ice mummies?

Digging through the permafrost was very difficult physically and took a long time. We used picks and shovels, and the permafrost was just like cement. We could not chip the ice surrounding the bodies, as this would have damaged them, so we carefully melted the ice with water.

What was the most fascinating part of the process?

Still, to this day, the most fascinating thing about our whole experience on Beechey Island was the realization that we came face to face with members of this famous expedition from the middle of the 19th century. Our work truly felt like a forensic investigation of a modern mass disaster—but it actually occurred in a previous century.

Was Sir John Franklin's body ever found?
No, his body has never been found. Questions still remain about whether he was "buried at sea," whether his body was prepared for return to England for burial, or whether he was buried somewhere on the northwest coast of King William Island.

If the crew had enough food on board to last for years, why do you think they turned to cannibalism?
Once they made the decision to desert the ships stuck in the ice, they would have been able to carry only so much food with them. Unless they were able to hunt, or get enough food from any Inuit they ran into, they would have eventually run out of food and risked starvation.

If lead poisoning hadn't confused them, do you think the crew could have made it to safety?
Though we feel that lead played some role in the disaster, we're unclear on its exact influence on the situation. Perhaps we will never know the whole story, but as time goes on and others continue investigating the disaster, we will get more detailed insight into many aspects of the circumstances leading to the loss of these explorers.

CHAPTER THREE

Viking Vinland

History Mystery

The first European explorer to set foot in North America was probably happy to see land after sailing for weeks in the Atlantic. He might have felt that he had finally arrived in a place of great potential, with trees and wheat, and even wild grapes. Who was he? Many historians and archaeologists believe he was a Viking named Leif Ericsson. If the legends are true, he beat Christopher Columbus to North America by about five hundred years.

Stories about Leif Ericsson were passed down from generation to generation among Norse people until finally, about eight hundred years ago, they were written down in long tales called sagas. *The Greenlander's Saga* and *The Saga of Erik the Red* both mention Leif leaving Greenland and sailing west to a place he named Vinland.

According to the sagas, Vinland, or Wine Land, got its name from the grapes that grew there. The wild grapevines were everywhere, and the Vikings said these grapes made the best wine they had ever tasted. They found a type of wild wheat they could use for bread, and they also found lots of trees. The Vikings' settlement in Greenland had plenty of rock, but few trees, so wood for boats and buildings was very valuable to the Vikings. In Vinland, they could load up on lumber and bring it back to Greenland.

But was Vinland just a mythical place of legends, or was it real? And if so, where was it?

Row, Row, Row Your Knarr?

In 1998, twelve men set sail in an exact copy of a Viking ship called a knarr. This was the same type of ship Leif Ericsson would have used. They built the knarr the same way the Vikings would have built theirs, using oak, pine, tamarack, locust wood, and iron rivets. It had only one square sail and some oars. The deck was open, so there was no protection from the weather. Vikings were hardy travellers! The knarr, christened *Snorri* (opposite), included modern navigational equipment, which was only to be used in an emergency. The crew wanted to cross the Atlantic Ocean using the same tools as the Vikings: the Sun and the stars. The Viking Voyage 1000 team landed safely in L'Anse aux Meadows on 22 September 1998, making the *Snorri* the first Viking ship to have made the trip from Greenland to Newfoundland by sail alone in more than six hundred years!

Puzzle Pieces

Researchers realized that by finding Vinland they could prove that the Vikings beat the other European explorers in discovering North America by hundreds of years and that the sagas were not just legends but travel logs.

In the 1960s, explorer Helge Ingstad found the remains of a settlement on the tip of Newfoundland's Northern Peninsula, at a place called L'Anse aux Meadows. The bumps and ridges in the ground here were typical of Norse sod houses and turned out to be the remains of the walls of eight buildings. Archaeologists found pieces of wood, iron nails, and pottery that they were able to carbon date to the 11th century, hundreds of years before Christopher Columbus began his explorations. The discovery of a possible Norse settlement at L'Anse aux Meadows, Newfoundland, caused a sensation. This was the first real proof scientists had that the sagas were more than myths and that the Vikings were the first to discover and settle North America.

Well, the mystery of the location of Vinland was not solved with the discovery of the settlement at L'Anse aux Meadows.

If the sagas were fact and not fiction, some things didn't fit. Wild grapes do not grow in Newfoundland, and the Northern Peninsula does not have thick forests—the land around L'Anse aux Meadows is marshy and grassy.

Among the northern islands of Newfoundland lies evidence, such as whalebone spades and spun yarn, that suggests the Vikings travelled between Greenland and the Canadian Arctic for generations.

E. WORKSHOP
ATELIER

Many anthropologists believe that the settlement at L'Anse aux Meadows was just Leif Ericsson's camp. It may have been used as a gateway to Vinland, which would have been farther south. This could explain the butternuts found at L'Anse aux Meadows. Butternuts grow in hardwood forests, where there is a long and warm summer. The closest places where they could grow wild are along the St. Lawrence River and on the coast of New Brunswick. Did Leif and his crew bring the butternuts from Vinland to their camp at L'Anse aux Meadows?

Even more exciting for researchers: other descriptions of Vinland from the sagas seem like they could be describing these parts of New Brunswick. Eastern New Brunswick has long, sandy beaches. Along the shores is a type of dune grass known as meal flour. Is this the wild wheat the Vikings mentioned?

Lost and Found

The artifacts found at L'Anse aux Meadows give archaeologists important information about the site's potential as a Viking camp. The bronze cloak pin found there was of Norse design. Cloak pins were used to hold clothing fabric together for both men and women. The spindle whorl and bone needle found at the site suggest women also stayed there, because in Viking culture only women weaved and sewed.

21

This replica of a longhouse at L'Anse aux Meadows National Park was made by stacking strips of sod that weighed 23 kg (50 lb.) each.

What Now?

No Viking settlements have been found south of L'Anse aux Meadows, but researchers have found evidence of more Viking visits in another part of Canada. Two hundred kilometres (124 mi.) south of Iqaluit on Baffin Island are the remains of a seven-hundred-year-old Norse shelter. Archaeologists have also found Norse-style spun yarn, decorated wood items, stones used for sharpening knives and axes, and even a whalebone spade.

Researchers are still looking for evidence that the Vikings travelled farther down the east coast to New England and beyond. Vikings were important traders in their time, exchanging goods all the way from the North Sea to the Mediterranean Sea. If the Vikings were exploring the East Coast of North America, scientists would expect to find more Norse items that were traded with the aboriginal people who lived along the coast. So far, no evidence has been found along the East Coast, but researchers are still looking.

Ask an Expert

NAME: Dr. Birgitta Wallace
TITLE: Archaeologist Emeritus
FROM: Parks Canada

What kind of evidence would prove whether or not a site was Vinland?
One single site could not be Vinland because Vinland was a vast region, not one particular spot. To prove that a site was in Vinland there must be physical evidence that the Norse people were once there and were able to grow wild grapes in the site's woods.

How do researchers know how many people lived at L'Anse aux Meadows?
The layout of the houses the Norse lived in during the 11th century in Iceland and Greenland is well known from many excavations over the years. People slept on wooden platforms running along the walls of the houses. One can get an idea of how many people could have lived in a house by counting the number of people who could fit on these platforms.

Is anyone searching the coast of New Brunswick for signs of Vinland?
As far as I know, nobody is searching the New Brunswick coast for signs of Vinland. When Vikings made trips to gather wood and food, they did not stay in one spot but moved around. In such situations they lived in tents or in booths. Booths had walls of sod and roofs of tent cloth. After a thousand years have passed, such buildings do not leave much or any trace in nature. That said, archaeologists working on other projects in New Brunswick know of the Norse visits and are keeping their eyes open.

Some people believe that the sagas describe the West Coast of Canada. Could the Vikings have made it that far?
There is not a chance that a Viking ship would have ventured as far from home as the West Coast. Viking ships were seaworthy, but even the voyage to Greenland from Norway was considered dangerous, and the sagas are full of tales of shipwrecks. When in L'Anse aux Meadows, the Norse were already as far away from their home as they were from Norway when at home in Greenland.

CHAPTER FOUR

Little Chicago

The Prairie town of Moose Jaw, Saskatchewan, is known as The Friendly City. In the past, it was a hub for the many smaller rural towns in the surrounding area and was known for its mineral spas and important railway junction.

But Moose Jaw has a darker history, one that includes gangsters engaged in hidden criminal activities and persecuted immigrants trying not to be noticed. Where can you hide on the flat, open prairie? Underground.

Since the 1920s, rumours persisted that under the streets of Moose Jaw is a network of tunnels that start from the old Canadian Pacific Railway station on Manitoba Street and run all the way up Main Street, as well as over a block or two on each side. It is said that the tunnels were home to persecuted Chinese immigrants and even used by the infamous gangster Al Capone.

Many Chinese immigrants used the tunnels as living space because they often had nowhere else to live as they struggled to pay the expensive head tax charged by the government. Many of the immigrants were also trying to escape the ill treatment they received by those who accused them of taking jobs from other Canadians.

If Al Capone used the tunnels, he used them for very different reasons. During Prohibition, he would have taken advantage of the direct railway line from Moose Jaw into Chicago to move illegal alcohol and to use the city as a hideout when he needed to get away from the police in Chicago.

In the years after Prohibition, however, many of the tunnels weren't used as much as before and most were sealed off. City officials denied any knowledge of them or the dark history associated with them.

But all this changed in the 1980s when construction workers on Main Street came upon sections of the tunnels while they were digging around buildings in the older part of downtown Moose Jaw. After this, it was very difficult to deny the existence of the tunnels.

The tunnels were real, but were the stories about Al Capone? Was Moose Jaw really "Little Chicago"?

Once, a secret entrance behind the Maple Leaf Hotel, now called the Cornerstone Inn, was the heart of the network of tunnels.

During Prohibition, many amateurs tried to make their own alcohol with homemade stills—highly dangerous operations often producing poisonous liquor and causing explosive fires.

Puzzle Pieces

The tunnels that run under Moose Jaw were originally built for practical use. Because of several fires in the 1800s, all new buildings in Moose Jaw had to be made of brick, not wood, and heated with boilers in basement rooms. Due to a shortage of boilermen, a group of building owners would hire one man to service several different boilers. To make it easier for the boilermen to get around, especially in the freezing winters of Manitoba, tunnels were built to connect the basements.

After the extremely high head tax was imposed, many Chinese immigrants worked and even raised their families underground in hidden rooms not used by the boilermen. And then, in the 1920s, the tunnels and their forgotten entrances, storerooms, and living quarters caught the eyes of the bootleggers.

The tunnels of Moose Jaw were set up perfectly for storing, shipping, and selling liquor. The fact that the tunnels went right to the train station meant that liquor could be moved without ever taking it above ground, where it could be seen by police or Temperance League members. The Canadian Pacific Railway depot in Moose Jaw was even a stop on the Soo Line, a rail line that headed directly south to Chicago.

One of the biggest players selling alcohol illegally during Prohibition was Al Capone. His headquarters were in Chicago. Residents said he visited Moose Jaw several times when things became too risky for him in the States. He would travel under a false name, and when in Moose Jaw, he would use the tunnels to stay out of sight until things cooled down.

No Drinking Allowed

Ratified in 1906, the Prohibition Act of Manitoba was supposed to reduce crime by keeping citizens sober and responsible by outlawing all forms of alcohol. Groups like the Temperance League thought they had rid society of a vicious evil. In fact, all the Act did was drive it underground. Literally.

The Chinese immigrants who lived in the tunnels were often already used to difficult living conditions. Many had worked on the railway, living in thin tents with little food and no medicine.

Al Who?

Al Capone often used the alias Al Brown when he didn't want to be noticed. Was this the same Al Brown who had an appointment in an old dentist's ledger from Moose Jaw?

A Price on Your Head

As many as seventeen thousand Chinese immigrants came to Canada in the 1880s to build the Canadian Pacific Railway. Many Canadians who had trouble finding work in 1885 blamed the Chinese immigrants who stayed on after the railway was finished. The government bent to the pressure and started a head tax. Each immigrant who wanted to stay had to pay $50. This was an enormous amount of money a hundred years ago. Still, many stayed and paid the tax. The government kept raising the amount, though, until it reached $500—more than a year's wages for most workers at the time. After this, many Chinese immigrants went underground to live in the tunnels and avoid the exorbitant tax.

Re-enactors from the Tunnels of Moose Jaw demonstrate the dangers of the tunnels in the 1920s. Boilers exploded, diseases spread in cramped living spaces, and an illegal alcohol industry brought gangsters with machine guns.

What Now?

Since the tunnels were rediscovered in the 1980s, a section of them has been opened for tourists. The rooms have been recreated to look like they did in the 1920s and tours give an idea of what life would have been like in them.

Other parts of the tunnel system have been found as older buildings are renovated or torn down. Some sections of the tunnels have been filled in because they are not stable and are a safety hazard.

Researchers are looking for documents and artifacts that can shed more light on the use of the tunnels under Moose Jaw. No official records have been found yet showing that Al Capone ever visited or stayed in Moose Jaw. Skeptics say that's because he was never there. Believers say that if he was hiding, he certainly wouldn't have signed a hotel register with his real name.

There is proof, however, that Capone was doing business in Saskatchewan. Court records in Regina show that he was sued by gangster Dutch Schultz. It seems Schultz was upset about a shipment of sixty cases of bad liquor. The court documents state that the case was withdrawn when Capone refunded Schultz his money.

Ask an Expert

NAME: Kelly Carty
TITLE: Cast Director
FROM: The Tunnels of Moose Jaw

Who were some of the people who say they saw Al Capone in Moose Jaw?
There was Ken Turner, who met him in the Brunswick Hotel, and Ken's father, who was on the Soo Line train with Capone once. As a boy, Jack Tillison remembers delivering telegrams in the tunnels and getting a big tip from Capone. And I do know that we have researched a story about Dr. Hugh Morris Young, who lanced Al Capone's tonsils.

Why did city officials deny the existence of the tunnels for so long?
They are and were common knowledge to anyone who grew up here, so I would assume it was because some people would rather not admit that Moose Jaw has a dark past. We now seem to embrace our history, as denying certainly does not make it go away.

Why did the police not shut down the bootleggers?
The police force here in the 1920s was very crooked under the leadership of Chief Johnson, and the police themselves may have tipped the gangsters off and helped them avoid a police raid and arrest.

Did any other famous gangsters do business in Moose Jaw?
We have heard stories of Dutch Schultz having been in the area. There were also the Bronfman brothers, who founded the Seagram Company, the largest maker of alcoholic beverages in the world. But back in the 1920s, Samuel, Harry, Abe, and Allen Bronfman ran a "booze by mail" business during Prohibition.

CHAPTER FIVE

Canada's Stonehenge

History Mystery

On a vast Alberta prairie at dawn, the first rays of sun peek over the horizon and stretch across the open plain. They touch an arrangement of stones on a low hill. The stones are stacked to form the shape of a V. The sun's rays are only able to shine through the point at the bottom of the V on two separate days out of the whole year—the days of the true equinoxes on 17 March and 25 September.

Is this a coincidence? It doesn't look like it. One-tonne stones have somehow been lifted and propped up with smaller rocks to form this V shape. All the rocks in this formation seem to have been arranged by human hands.

The V rocks are not the only pattern of stones found near Majorville, Alberta. Nearby is a giant ring of stones about 28 m (92 ft.) across. In the centre stands a cairn, or large pile of rocks, which measures 9 m (30 ft.) across and 1.6 m (5 ft.) high. Scientists believe it was originally taller, about 2 m (7 ft.) high, but because of natural forces and vandalism its size has decreased. Lines of stones that look like spokes on a wheel radiate out from the cairn to touch an outer ring. When seen from above, the stone pattern looks like an image of the Sun.

Researchers found spearheads, arrowheads, bones, and other objects at the bottom of the cairn. Using carbon dating, scientists figured out the rough age of the Majorville cairn itself. The bone fragments showed that the stone circle was built about five thousand years ago. That makes this site older than Stonehenge in England *and* the pyramids in Egypt.

Although thousands of years old, the spokes of Canada's Stonehenge can still be seen under the prairie grass.

Carbon Dating

Carbon dating is a method of figuring out the age of organic material, such as wood, charcoal, seeds, hair, skin, and bone. Carbon-14 is a radioactive element found in all organic material, and scientists know how long it takes for the radioactivity of this element to decay. When researchers test a piece of organic material, they compare how much carbon-14 is left with how much the material originally had. This difference in carbon-14 content tells them roughly how many years old something is.

Stonehenge

Stonehenge, located in Wiltshire, England, has fascinated scientists for years. Without modern cranes or machines, many of the stones, some more than 50 tonnes (55 tons), were raised upright to form inner and outer circles. Massive rectangular stones were then placed flat on top of these upright stones, up to 6 m (20 ft.) from the ground. Scientists are still trying to figure out how ancient people accomplished this without any modern equipment, especially since some of the stones used to build Stonehenge came from a site in Wales about 300 km (187 mi.) away.

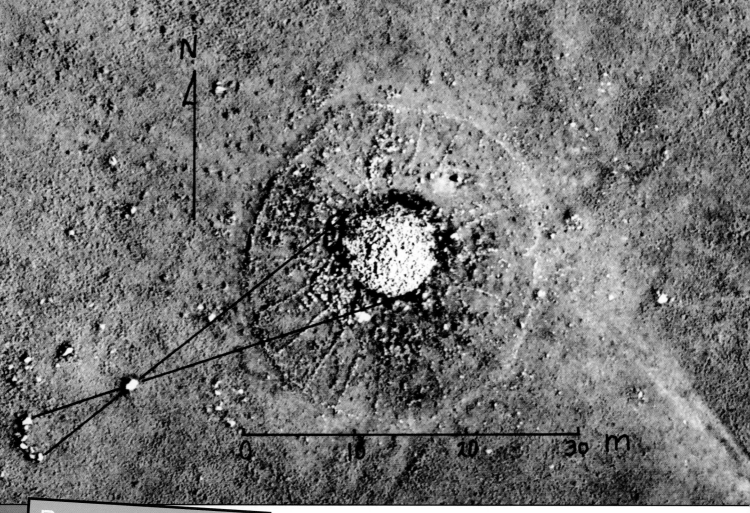

N

0   10   20   30 m

Puzzle Pieces

From above, it's easier to see the representations (left to right) of the crescent Moon, the morning star (Venus), and the Sun.

More than one hundred stone rings are spread out across the Prairies, some big, some small. What makes the Majorville site so unique is that the stones are placed in ways that signify astronomical signs and important days of the year. Some researchers believe this means the Majorville site was used as a solar or lunar calendar. While other stone rings across the Prairies may have been meeting grounds, used for dancing during ceremonies, or memorials to brave warriors, evidence at the Majorville site seems to point to another purpose. Here the placement of the rocks seems to create a calendar in stone.

The Oxbow people living on the Prairies five thousand years ago didn't have a printed calendar. They used the movement of the Sun, stars, and

Moon to mark changes in the seasons. Festivals and ceremonies were often tied to special days such as solstices and equinoxes. The carefully placed stone markers at the Majorville site seem to represent these important dates.

The Moon, morning star, and Sun are not only sacred symbols to many Plains aboriginal people, but are also represented in stones at the Majorville site. As the morning star rose above the horizon, it symbolized a new beginning for Plains aboriginal people. The Sun and the Moon were circles that represented life with no beginning and no end.

Researchers, like Dr. Gordon Freeman of the University of Alberta, are sure that the V rocks at the Majorville site mark the two true equinoxes. This means that the people who built the solar temple would have used these V rocks to keep track of the months of the year and the seasons.

Equinox means "equal night." The spring equinox and the fall equinox, which are the true equinoxes, mark the days when daylight and nighttime hours are equal. In North America, there are twelve hours of daylight and twelve hours of darkness on 17 March and 25 September.

Solstice means "Sun stands still." The winter solstice marks the day with the fewest hours of daylight and the summer solstice is the day with the most daylight hours. In Canada, our winter solstice is on 21 December. After this date, the days begin to get longer until 20 or 21 June, the time of the summer solstice.

It was at the time of the sumer solstice that Plains aboriginal people held their Sun Dance ceremony. It was a ceremony of celebration that lasted about four days. It began with fasting and included special dances, passed down from generation to generation, which showed how all of nature is intertwined.

The shape of the point and the location of the notches are clues that help researchers date arrowheads. This one is roughly five thousand years old.

Ancient Architects

Scientists are not sure who built the Majorville structures or any of the other stone rings. Spearheads that were made by the Oxbow people who lived on the Prairies four to five thousand years ago were found in some of the cairns. But scientists aren't sure whether the Oxbow people built the original stone circles or just added to even older structures that were already there.

Stone Circles

Stone rings can be found on every continent on Earth except Antarctica, probably because in many cultures the circle is a mystical symbol. In some cultures it represents the Sun, the source of energy from which all life begins. To the Plains aboriginal people, life was thought of as a sacred cycle, from birth to death. The circle is a motif often found in Plains aboriginal artwork and tool designs. If they were the builders of the solar temple, as many researchers believe they were, then it makes sense that they would have used a circle motif, since this symbol was an important and necessary part of everyday life on the Prairies thousands of years ago.

The empty space between the rocks forms a V shape that, when the sun shines through, pinpoints the days of the spring and fall equinoxes.

What Now?

In order to learn more about the meaning and history of the
Majorville site, researchers are talking to First Nations elders.
Plains aboriginal people typically pass down their history orally,
through stories, songs, and dances. If more people understand
this culture and heritage, more people will understand why these
sites are so important to study and preserve.

Ask an Expert

NAME: Dr. Gordon Freeman
TITLE: Professor Emeritus
FROM: University of Alberta
Author of *Canada's Stonehenge: Astounding Archaeological Discoveries in Canada, England, and Wales*

How did you realize that the rocks were placed carefully by humans and were not just left behind by glaciers or other natural causes?
I have studied patterns my whole career, and I recognized a pattern in the stones as soon as I got near the site. Also, some of the rocks were chipped and shaped to create notches so they could be stacked in particular ways.

What can stone rings teach us today?
They tell us that there was genius on the Prairies five thousand years ago. And there were Plains aboriginal people as smart as Albert Einstein.

Are all stone rings solar or lunar calendars?
No, many rings are stones that anchored the bottoms of tipi covers, and some rings are grave markers. There are two other sites that I think have time-measurement information in them. Originally I was going to investigate them when I was finished with the Majorville site, but now I think that will be a job for the next generation.

Have you found any new information recently?
I still go out to the Majorville site and am still doing calculations and discovering more lines and patterns that have meaning. Just recently I found the individual years in the four-year leap-year cycle accurately marked with stone lines.

How can we help protect sacred sites in Canada?
By not touching any stones at or near these sites. When we move a stone, we destroy information, even if we think we are putting the stone down exactly where it was. Governments need to understand the importance of these sites and give official protection to them.

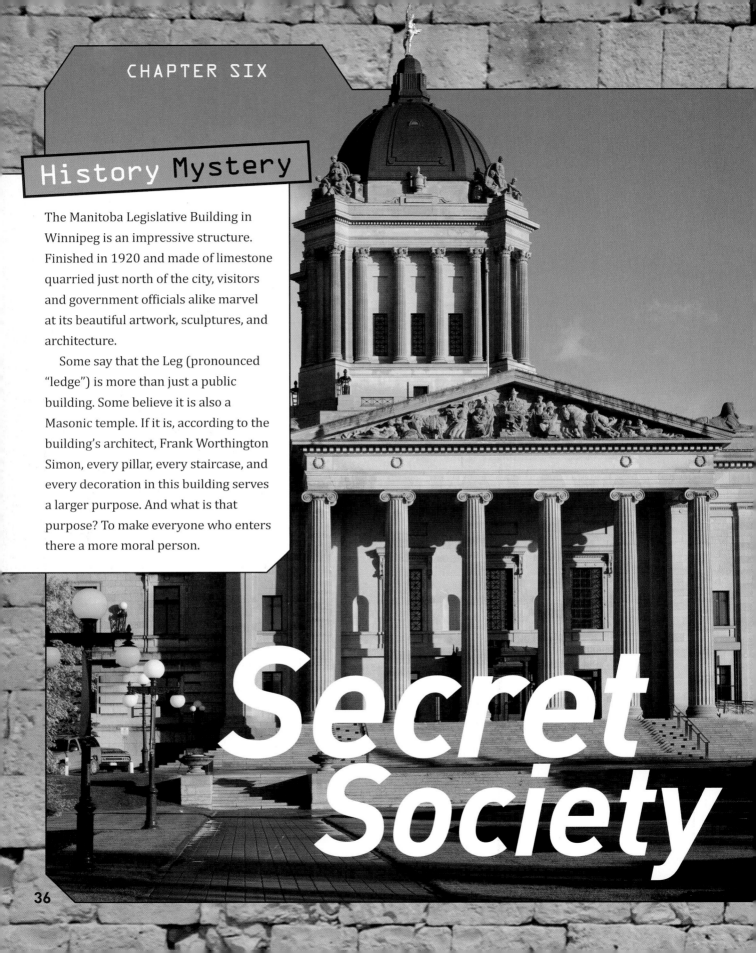

CHAPTER SIX

History Mystery

The Manitoba Legislative Building in Winnipeg is an impressive structure. Finished in 1920 and made of limestone quarried just north of the city, visitors and government officials alike marvel at its beautiful artwork, sculptures, and architecture.

Some say that the Leg (pronounced "ledge") is more than just a public building. Some believe it is also a Masonic temple. If it is, according to the building's architect, Frank Worthington Simon, every pillar, every staircase, and every decoration in this building serves a larger purpose. And what is that purpose? To make everyone who enters there a more moral person.

Secret Society

The Freemasons is an organization for men that has existed for hundreds of years, maybe longer. Freemasonry is connected to builders of medieval Europe, but members are sworn to secrecy and can't discuss what happens during meetings and ceremonies. Freemasons take an oath not to tell outsiders about the group's signs, tokens, or handshakes. In public, the secret society does charity work, such as giving medical care to and educating people in need and building shelters and hospitals.

Ancient Builders

Freemasons have their roots in the ancient stonemasons guild. The word "Freemason" is a shortened version of "freestone mason." Freestone masons were skilled craftsmen who could "freely" sculpt stone and built some of the world's most famous and lasting structures, such as cathedrals, temples, walls, monuments, bridges, and aqueducts. In medieval times, young stonemasons served as apprentices for seven years. During this time, the master stonemasons, who had to study their craft's tradition for thirty years, would pass on their knowledge and skill.

Freemasons believe in the power of symbols, metaphors, and architecture. The Leg was designed to help the people entering it think and act in a better way. But would a government in Canada knowingly build a Masonic temple as its legislative building?

Well, the architect was a Freemason. The committee that selected his design was made up of Freemasons, too. And all the builders they hired? That's right...Freemasons. On top of this, the cabinet of the ruling provincial government at the time was also made up of Freemasons.

Is it possible that Simon cleverly hid the symbols and messages of Freemasonry in the structure and decoration of the building? The general public and later members of Parliament would have had no idea that as they walked through the Leg, they were actually participating in a Masonic ritual meant to illuminate their minds and uplift their spirits.

Built under the rule of King Solomon, Solomon's Temple is said to have sat on Temple Mount in ancient Jerusalem.

Puzzle Pieces

But how can a building make you a better person? Well, the Freemasons believe that geometry and symbols carry meaning and power. Freemasons often use Egyptian symbols, such as pyramids, sphinxes, and hieroglyphs, to show their link with this ancient culture. They believe that Freemasonry began with Adam in the Bible and continued on with an Egyptian priest named Hermes Trismegistus, who brought picture writing, or hieroglyphics, to Egypt. Some say that the "Golden Boy" statue at the very top of the Leg dome represents this ancient Egyptian.

Freemasons also believe that the most important and mystical building ever made was Solomon's Temple. If the Leg is truly a monument of Freemasonry, it would be modelled on this ancient and sacred three-roomed building.

Does the Leg have a porch or entrance guarded by two beasts? Check. The two bison in the main entrance room stand at the bottom of the staircase. Does it have a Holy Place with an altar?

Check again. The Rotunda has a circular railing that is open to the room below. What about the most sacred room in Solomon's Temple—the Holy of Holies, where the Ark of the Covenant was kept behind blue curtains? Yes. Just past the Rotunda is a set of double doors that leads to a small room called the Lieutenant-Governor's Reception Room. This room and the Holy of Holies are the same size: twenty cubits by twenty cubits. Blue curtains hang from the large windows, just like in Solomon's Temple. What about the Ark, the chest that held the two stone tablets inscribed with the Ten Commandments? Is it there? Well, if you look out the window and up on the roof, you will see a stone sculpture of the Ark.

The Egyptian sphinxes and the Golden Boy statue of Hermes that decorate the outside of the Leg are symbols used by the Freemasons to provide protection and guidance for those who enter.

By the Numbers

In Freemasonry, certain numbers have mystical significance. In the Manitoba Leg, the numbers three, five, eight, and thirteen hold special meaning and are used again and again in the building's architecture and decoration. The Leg is full of these numbers. Staircases are often in three sections and benches and lamps often have three legs. Certain mouldings, archways, and flower decorations come in groups of five. There are eight columns in the portico, eight lamps between the columns, and eight points on the Pool of the Black Star. Seats, steps, and lights come in thirteens.

Everything so far points to the Leg being more than just another government building. But have we uncovered everything the Freemasons may have worked into its design?

The number three holds special meaning for Freemasons, who have three degrees, or levels, of membership.

The Long and the Short of It

The cubit is an ancient measurement that was used to measure such things as cloth, rope, wood, and buildings. It was also used in the construction of temples and other ancient architecture. A cubit is roughly the length of an average adult's arm from fingertip to elbow, which is about 45 cm (18 in.).

Ask an Expert

NAME: Frank Albo
TITLE: Historian
FROM: University of Cambridge
Author of *The Hermetic Code: Unlocking One of Manitoba's Greatest Mysteries*

How was the Lieutenant-Governor's Reception Room discovered?

It was discovered in an obsessive hunt to uncover the mysteries of the building's architecture and the motivation behind the architect's design.

Why is the Room kept locked?

The Lieutenant-Governor's Reception Room is kept locked and can only be opened by security or from inside by the staff of the Lieutenant-Governor of Manitoba. The official explanation is because of the delicate hand-woven carpet on the floor inside the room, but it is also because the architect intended it to be a replication of the Holy of Holies of Solomon's Temple, the most sacred room in which the Ark of the Covenant was kept.

What Now?

There is one more mystery of the Leg that has not been solved to this day.

The floor below the open circular railing "altar" has a beautiful tiled pattern on it. It is an eight-pointed star called the Pool of the Black Star. Beneath this star is a mysterious chamber. Researchers haven't been able to determine why it was built or what is inside.

Many researchers have tried for years to gain access to the room to investigate but have had no success. The Leg still has some secrets to keep.

The centre of the Rotunda (opposite) is open to the floor below, directly over the Pool of the Black Star (above).

Do you think there are codes and messages hidden in the decoration and architecture?
Yes, the building is full of sophisticated geometric and symbolic codes. The architect, F.W. Simon, was the Grand Architect of Scottish Freemasonry, and he envisioned the Manitoba Legislative Building as a "temple of democracy" that in the course of time would make people more intelligent, balanced, and altogether more civilized human beings.

Do you feel any different when you go inside?
I think when properly understood, the building helps impart lessons in morality, mysticism, ancient architecture, and the history of world civilization.

Sacred Destination

The Freemasons have been linked to the building of many famous sites. One of the most famous is Rosslyn Chapel in Scotland. The small chapel is on land owned by the Sinclair family, many of whom were Grand Masters of Scottish Freemasonry over hundreds of years. Some of the carvings inside the chapel seem to show crops that were not known in Europe at the time it was built, and they also show mysterious cubes with patterns on them that some researchers say are musical notes. Among the many carvings and images are an eight-pointed star and what looks like a man being initiated into the Freemasons.

CHAPTER SEVEN

The Great Lakes were formed after the last ice age when meltwater filled the basins carved out by the glaciers.

The First of Many

Le Griffon (or *The Griffin*) was the first schooner to sail the Great Lakes. In September 1679, at only a little over a year old, the schooner was sailing from Green Bay in upper Lake Huron when she disappeared. Her wreck has never been found. The Great Lakes Triangle had claimed its first victim.

Great Lakes Triangle

On 28 October 1870, Captain John Burrill prepared the schooner *St. James* to set sail from Toledo, Ohio. He had spent most of his life on the Great Lakes and looked forward to a smooth trip with his crew of six to deliver the fourteen thousand bushels of wheat stored in the schooner's hold. Fine weather was forecast for their trip across Lake Erie, through the Welland Canal, and into Lake Ontario.

A few days later, the *St. James* and everyone aboard disappeared. When the schooner failed to turn up at the Welland Canal, word spread quickly that she was missing. Ships up and down busy Lake Erie kept a watch for her crew, but they were never seen again. Those who lived nearby and sailed on the lakes believed the *St. James* was another victim of the Great Lakes Triangle.

Since ships first sailed on the waters, there have been mysterious disasters and disappearances on the Great Lakes. This area has had a higher concentration of unexplainable ship and plane disappearances than anywhere else in the world...even more than the Bermuda Triangle!

The Bermuda Triangle

The points of the triangle are roughly Bermuda, Puerto Rico, and the tip of Florida. The Bermuda Triangle is a zone notorious for ship and plane disappearances. One of the most famous cases is the disappearance of five U.S. bombers from Fort Lauderdale, Florida, on a training flight in December 1945. The planes and their crews were never found. Even more mysterious is the fact that the search-and-rescue plane sent after them also disappeared.

43

Puzzle Pieces

One hundred years after it was lost, divers exploring the wrecks in Lake Erie found the shipwreck of the *St. James*. But instead of providing answers to what had happened, their discovery only deepened the mystery.

The schooner was found sitting upright on the bottom of the lake and its rigging showed that the sails had been up when it sank. When a bad storm hits, the sails are lowered, so this meant there was no storm the day the boat sank. There were no holes in the hull and no broken masts. In fact, divers could not find any damage at all. What could have caused a perfectly sound ship to sink into the lake in good weather? Lake Erie may have given up the *St. James*, but it wasn't giving up all its secrets.

Researchers have noticed that some parts of the Great Lakes have strange magnetic forces that interfere with equipment, especially in bad weather. If a ship's captain is unable to rely on radar or GPS, or even a compass, the ship and her crew might be in real danger. Take the example of the *Eliza Quinlan*.

This schooner was loaded with coal in Oswego, New York, and headed for Napanee, Ontario, on a course that would take it straight through what is called the Marysburgh Vortex. In this area, located on Lake Ontario, the weather is often foggy and stormy, and some people believe compasses are particularly prone to fail here. All these factors came into play for the *Eliza Quinlan*: a heavy fog and snow made it hard to see, and the ship's compass wasn't working properly. The schooner ran aground on a sandbar far south of where the captain thought he was. The men were saved, but huge waves pounded the stranded ship until she broke up.

These images taken from a video shot by divers exploring the wreck of the *St. James* show how well the ship's structure has held up.

Vanished!

In 1937, while sailing on Lake Michigan, Captain George R. Donner went to rest in his cabin on the freighter *McFarland*. He told an officer to wake him when they were near Port Washington. When the crew member went to find him, the door was locked and there was no answer. When the officer unlocked the door, he found an empty room. The crew searched the entire ship but found no trace of him. Captain Donner had disappeared.

Special Measures

The mysterious disappearances on the Great Lakes have not only caused problems for ships, but also for planes flying over them. More than forty planes have gone missing over or near the lakes. With so many crashes and disappearances, new safety rules have been created. Pilots flying over some parts of the Great Lakes have to file a special flight plan called the "Lake Reporting Service" plan. As the plane flies over the lake, the pilot must check in every ten minutes. If a pilot doesn't report after fifteen minutes, search and rescue will begin immediately.

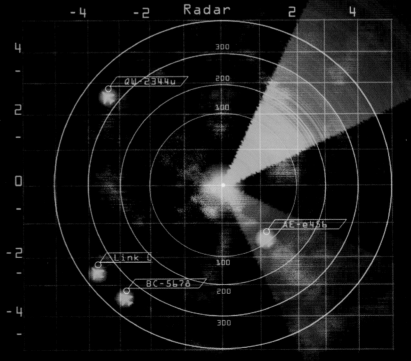

What Now?

Researchers are trying to understand what it is about the Great Lakes that makes them so dangerous to ships and planes.

If magnetic forces are the reason, then researchers hope to find an explanation in the geology of the area. The magnetic disturbances near Kingston, Ontario, for instance, may be related to an unusual depression found in the lakebed. Scientists wonder if it's a crater formed by a meteor millions of years ago. The round shape, the raised rim, and the sloping sides all point to something smashing into the Earth. A meteor could easily have been made of material that would cause the compass problems in the area.

The magnetic oddity is not limited to eastern Lake Ontario. The U.S. Geological Survey charts show that there are magnetic deviations on Lake Huron, Lake Erie, Lake Michigan, and Lake Superior as well. Were captains being drawn to their deaths by unreliable compass readings?

Shipwreck explorers are using new technology to find and identify sunken ships in the Great Lakes. They hope that wrecks will provide clues to how they sank. Many of the shipwrecks lie hundreds of feet underwater. Most divers don't go deeper than 41 m (135 ft.), so remotely operated vehicles (ROVs) are used to find and examine deep shipwrecks.

A compass needle naturally points to the magnetic north pole. If anything disturbs this reading, the user can become hopelessly lost.

Ask an Expert

NAME: Mark Bourrie
TITLE: Journalist
FROM: Carleton University
Author of *Many a Midnight Ship: True Stories of Great Lakes Shipwrecks*

Are Great Lakes storms as bad as those at sea?
Yes. Winds on the lakes can reach hurricane force, especially in the fall. Lake waves are different from sea waves: they are much closer together and much steeper. Summer squalls—short, violent storms that appear quickly—are common and are responsible for many boating deaths. Jacques Cousteau, the great marine scientist who invented scuba gear and sailed around the world making marine documentaries, once said that a fall storm in northern Georgian Bay, just off Lake Huron, was the most frightening weather he had ever seen.

What can the shipwrecks tell us?
Many of the Great Lakes ship stories show what happens when people are put into dramatic and dangerous situations. We can learn a lot about human nature by seeing their reactions. As well, we can learn a lot about the settlement of the Great Lakes region, about old technology, and about the histories of transportation and industry.

Is it legal to take things from shipwrecks in the Great Lakes?
No. The wrecks are usually private property. They belong to the people who owned the ships, or to their insurance companies. Wrecks whose ownership is unknown belong to the province of Ontario. Unfortunately, that doesn't always stop people from taking artifacts.

Would you feel safe sailing on or flying over the Great Lakes?
I feel as safe on the Great Lakes as on any other body of water, though I don't like boats or planes much. The higher safety standards are one of the reasons why there hasn't been a ship lost since 1975. That's a record. Before the 1950s, it was normal for at least three ships to be lost every year, and some years ten or more ships were lost.

INDEX

Acknowledgements

This book would not have been possible without the wonderful Canadian researchers, professors, historians, and authors who so generously gave their time, knowledge, and photographs. Many thanks to Frank Albo, Richard Armstrong, Charles Barkhouse, Dr. Owen Beattie, Mark Bourrie, Kelly Carty, Dr. Gordon Freeman, the late Dr. David Kelley, Dr. Patricia Sutherland, and Dr. Birgitta Wallace. I hope I was able to capture the passion and excitement they feel for their work.

Special thanks to fellow writers Kelly Milner Halls, for answering all my questions with her non-fiction expertise, and Hélène Boudreau, for reading early drafts of the manuscript.

Sincere thanks to everyone at Owlkids Books for their hard work and dedication in bringing this book to young readers.

As always, heartfelt thanks to Craig, Alex, Chelsey, Nathan, and Haley for their unfailing love and support.

Consultants

Frank Albo, University of Cambridge; Richard Armstrong, En'owkin Centre; Charles Barkhouse, Friends of Oak Island; Dr. Owen Beattie, University of Alberta; Mark Bourrie, Carleton University; Kelly Carty, Tunnels of Moose Jaw; D.J. Fife, Petroglyphs Provincial Park; Dr. Gordon Freeman, University of Alberta; Dr. David H. Kelley, University of Calgary; Dr. Patricia Sutherland, Museum of Civilization; Dr. Birgitta Wallace, Parks Canada

Photos

Linda Ross, 6; Public Domain, 7 (Captain William Kidd), 13 (Sir John Franklin), 27, 42–43 (maps); Charles Barkhouse, 8–10; Owen Beattie, reprinted with permission from *Frozen in Time: The Fate of the Franklin Expedition* (Toronto: Douglas & McIntyre, 2004), 12, 14; Steve Ebbert, 13 (graves), 16; Russell Kaye, 18, 21–22; Moose Jaw Public Library, 25 (Main Street); Chicago History Museum, 25 (still); Royal BC Museum, 26; Tunnels of Moose Jaw, 28; Cliff LeSergent, 30; James King-Holmes, Science Photo Library, 31 (carbon dating); Gordon Freeman, 32, 33 (cairn), 34; BLM Montana/Dakotas, 33 (spear point); De Agostini, SuperStock, 38 (Solomon's Temple); Paul Armstrong, 38 (sphinx, Golden Boy), 39–40, 41 (Pool of the Black Star); Tom Wilson, 44

All other photos are royalty-free (iStockphoto, Dreamstime).